MILA BOUTAN

Art Activity Pack

"I learned all by myself"

Rousseau

Look at the leaves in this painting.
There are over twenty shades of green. These
deep colors invite you into the paintings of
Henri Rousseau. Rousseau was a painter most
famous for his images of tropical jungles. But
despite his exotic subject choice, Rousseau never
left France. He was a simple man who had never
actually been trained as a formal painter or
traveled to real jungles to see the beasts and
landscapes of his paintings. His tropical
scenes were all conjured up by his
vivid imagination.

Moi-même - Portrait paysage
(Myself - Landscape Portrait)
Prague, Narodni Gallery

Rousseau was not always a painter.
He was employed for twenty-three
years by the Octroi de Paris, a
government office that collected
taxes. His job was to check the
goods that came through Paris
and he was called the Douanier,
the Customs Officer. Because
many things arrived in Paris
by boat—building materials, coal,
wheat, wine—several of these offices
were located on the banks of the River
Seine. Rousseau loved the Seine—it
inspired him to paint. Rousseau began
by painting, quite naturally, what he

Vue de l'Ile Saint-Louis prise du Quai Henri IV.
(View of the Ile Saint-Louis Taken from Quai Henri IV)
The Phillips Collection, Washington

saw everyday... "What makes me happier than anything else is to contem-plate nature and to paint it... When I see the sun, the flowers, I say to myself: That's all mine!" Most of the famous artists of Rousseau's time studied for years at the School of Fine Arts. They learned by copying the paintings of the past and by listening to the modern masters, who worked slowly in the calm of their studios. In contrast, a new group of young painters, called Impressionists, preferred to take their easels outdoors and use bright colors freely. Rousseau became friendly with some of the Impressionists and adopted some of their ideas. More than painting realistic images, he wanted to paint images that would make viewers feel certain emotions. But even though he was influenced by the Impressionists, Rousseau was one of a kind. He didn't start painting until he was almost forty years old—painting only on evenings and Sundays. He had never studied painting. The little he knew about painting he learned by him-self. He worked by instinct.

Below and details: *View from the Pont de Grenelle* • Musée de Laval.

Magic and Mystery

Rousseau said, "When I see these strange plants from exotic countries, it seems that I enter a dream." The deep colors of plants and animals make his paintings feel mysterious. The people and animals look as if they are part of a magical world. The animals look like people, the people look like animals. The painting becomes like a living jungle—where sometimes even the plants look alive.

exotic flowers

wild animals

dense jungle

mysterious person

Jungles

In these paintings there are few clouds and no insects. Everything is orderly. In Rousseau's jungles we sometimes feel like beasts and flowers are hiding everywhere. Eyes are watching us from behind the bushes and trees. It feels as if the jungle is growing all around us. Notice that one way he makes the jungle feel so large is by creating a unique sense of perspective. Perspective is the way an artist shows distance in an image. If you were standing in a jungle, the leaves at the top of the trees would look smaller to you than those at the bottom. But Rousseau's leaves at the top of trees are often larger than the bottom leaves.

 ream or

Is the lion rocking the gypsy in her sleep? Or is it going to eat her? Perhaps it does not exist at all.

Perhaps it appears only in the young girl's dream. Because this scene is not realistic, it looks like a painting created to invent, to tell a story. It looks like paradise, with a perfect sky, a river that flows gently, a magical moon, and a dress cut out of a rainbow. The lion seems tame. It's almost a toy, like a teddy bear.

This famous picture, painted in 1897, was found in 1923, in Paris at a plumber's house. Most of the time, Rousseau had no money and so he paid for things with his paintings instead of money.

This painting captures a sense of Rousseau's ability to use magical moods and deep colors to shift perspective—the very things which made him famous in the art world for years to come.

Reality

The Sleeping Gypsy • © photo The Museum of Modern Art, New York • Gift of Mrs. Simon Guggenheim.

Henri Rousseau was born in 1844, in Laval, France. There is no known biography of him because he was not well known when he was alive. He was an average student in most subjects, but he excelled in drawing and music. He enjoyed playing the violin. When he was caught as an accomplice to a petty theft, he enlisted in the army to avoid going to prison. Later, he led people to believe that he had fought in the Mexican war, and that he had seen virgin forests and wild beasts! But the truth is that he never traveled outside of France. From 1871 on, he worked and lived in Paris. His wife gave birth to seven children; but only two survived.

In 1884, he decided to study paintings in the world famous French museum, the Louvre.

That is when art became a passion for him. He wanted to become a great painter. Despite his low income, he rented an artist's studio and, even with his little experience, exhibited his works at the Salon des Indépendants, where anyone could display canvases. His paintings were large (he used enormous canvases) and so they were noticed.

And nearly every year, until his death, he showed his paintings to the public. A few painters appreciated the quality of his colors. Many people made fun of him. They laughed and even danced in front of his paintings. They found them ridiculous. A famous writer even bought one of them for his Museum of Horrors! But

Rousseau made fun of those who teased him. He was convinced he was right. He went so far as to claim that he was the best among the painters of his time.

Eventually young writers started to say good things about Rousseau. Still, he sold very few paintings and the paintings he did sell, he sold for low prices. He was debt-ridden. In 1906, he met the famous poet Guillaume Apollinaire and painted his portrait. Two years later, a friend organized the first and only private showing of Rousseau's works. Unfortunately, no one came, because they forgot to write the address on the invitations! Young Picasso, who had bought a painting by Rousseau,

held a banquet at his studio in Rousseau's honor. Some American art lovers were present, and they helped establish Rousseau's reputation in the United States. He died in 1910. One third of his works disappeared, were destroyed or lost, because no one thought they had any value. A few paintings were found several decades after the painter's death. Today, he is respected all over the world.

ART CREDITS

BOOK: Cover and pages 10 (detail) and 11: *The Sleeping Gypsy*. © photo **The Museum of Modern Art, New York.** Gift of Mrs. Simon Guggenheim. • Page 1 (details): *The Dream.* © photo, **The Museum of Modern Art, New York.** Gift of Nelson A. Rockefeller • Page 2, left: *Myself—Landscape Portrait*. **National Gallery, Prague.** © photo Artephot/Held. Bottom: *View of the Ile Saint-Louis Taken From the Quai Henri IV.* **The Phillips Collection, Washington D.C.** © Edward Owen. • Page 3: *View from the Pont de Grenelle.* © **Musée de Laval.** photo Bernard Leportier. • Pages 4 and 5 (and details): *The Snake Charmer*. **Musée d'Orsay, Paris.** © photo R.M.N. • Page 6, details: *The Dream.* © photo **The Museum of Modern Art, New York.** Gift of Nelson A. Rockefeller. Top: *Repast of the Lion.* © photo **The Metropolitan Museum of Modern Art, New York.** Gift of Sam A. Lewisohn, 1951. Middle: *The Hungry Lion*. **Kuntsmuseum, Basel.** © photo Artephot/Babey. Bottom: *The Waterfall.* © photo 1994, **The Art Institute of Chicago.** • Page 7, top: *Black Man Attacked by a Jaguar*. **Kuntsmuseum, Basel.** © photo Lauros/ Giraudon. Middle: *The Dream.* © photo **The Museum of Modern Art, New York.** Gift of Nelson A. Rockefeller. Bottom: *The Flamingoes.* **Private collection, New York.** © photo R.M.N. • Pages 8 and 9: *Exotic Landscape*. **The Norton Simon Foundation, Pasadena, CA.** © photo Antoni E. Dolinski. • Pages 10 (lettering): *War.* **Musée d'Orsay, Paris.** © photo Lauros/Giraudon. • Pages 12 and 13 (biography): 1. *Self-portrait with a Lamp.* **Musée du Louvre, Paris.** © photo R.M.N. • 2. *The Poet and the Muse.* **Kuntsmuseum, Basel.** © photo Lauros/ Giraudon. • 3. *Portrait of Joseph Brummer.* **Kuntsmuseum, Basel.** © photo Artephot/Ideca. • 4. *The Bouquet of Flowers.* **Private collection, New York.** © photo Artephot/Ideca. • 5. *The Banks of the Bièvre Near Bicêtre, Spring.* © photo **The Metropolitan Museum of Modern Art, New York.** Gift of Marshall Field, 1939. • 6. *The Pink Candle.* **The Phillips Collection, Washington D.C.** © photo Edward Owen. • 7. *Ship in a Storm.* **Musée de l'Orangerie, Paris.** © photo Lauros/Giraudon.

WORKBOOK: Pages 2 and 3: *Exotic Landscape.* **The Norton Simon Foundation, Pasadena, CA.** © photo Antoni E. Dolinski. Page 4 (details), top: *The Hungry Lion.* **Kuntsmuseum, Basel.** © photo Artephot/Babey. Middle: *Repast of the Lion.* © photo **The Metropolitan Museum of Modern Art, New York.** Gift of Sam A. Lewisohn, 1951. Bottom: *The Waterfall.* © photo 1994, **The Art Institute of Chicago.**

chronicle books

85 Second Street, San Francisco, CA 94105
http://www.chronbooks.com

Distributed in Canada by
Raincoast Books, 8680 Cambie Street, Vancouver, B.C. V6P 6M9

10 9 8 7 6 5 4 3 2 1

ISBN: 0-8118-1691-5   © 1997 Mila Editions/Albin Michel   English translation © 1997 Chronicle Books
Published in North America by Chronicle Books   Printed in Spain

Rousseau

My Artist's Notebook

(with help from
Henri Rousseau)

mila boutan

Note to Young Artists

You have just looked at Rousseau's
jungles, now you are the artist!
This notebook is for painting
and drawing.
Paint directly on the pages
or make several paintings and glue
your favorites into the notebook.

A dense forest? ... A motionless bird? ... A doe standing still and listening? ... What can you draw to make me guess right away that you are thinking of Rousseau?

In the paintings by Rousseau, did
Flowers ... Giant cactus ...

Draw and color your own jungle while thinking

you notice the variety of tropical plants? Foliage ... Fruits ...
Pepper trees ... Sugar cane...

of Rousseau.

Henri Rousseau

Here are some animals
painted by Rousseau.

What are the wild animals living in
your own jungle?

Draw them ...

Animals

In Rousseau's jungles, did you see... a giraffe? A crocodile? A parrot? A scorpion?

Draw other animals that

Rousseau has forgotten to draw...

Exotic fruits

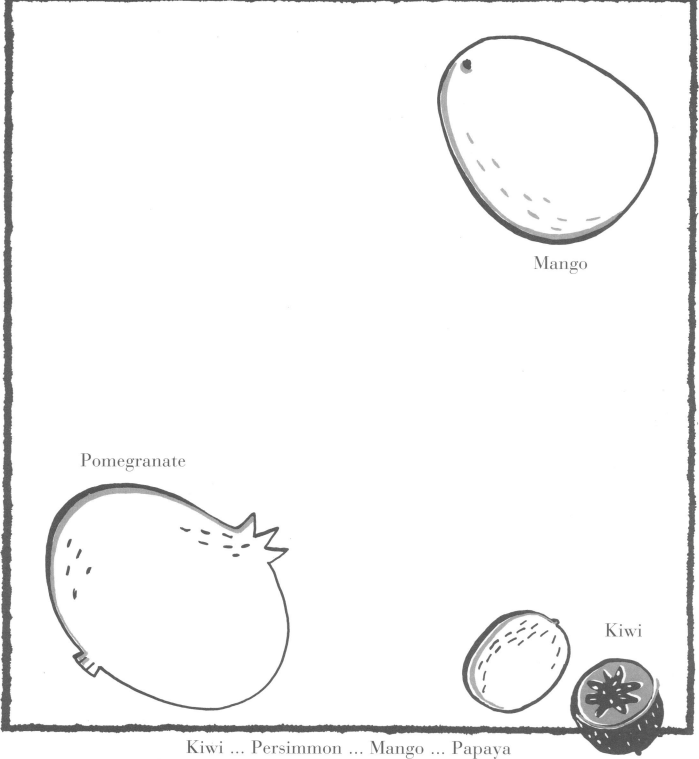

Mango

Pomegranate

Kiwi

Kiwi ... Persimmon ... Mango ... Papaya

Do you know other exotic fruits? Draw and color them ...

A Word Game

exotic, mysterious, sketches, joy, soft curves, volume, island, spirituality, travel, impression, spots of light, freedom, jungles, drawing, nature, empty space, light, touch, dream, ballerina, composition, bright harmonies, wild, pure colors, festive, happiness, gracefulness, harshness, sculpture, movement, wild beasts.

ISBN: 0-8118-1691-5
© 1996 Mila Editions/Albin Michel
Based on the original French text by Mila Boutan, Pascale Estellon, Anne Weiss, Yves Véquaud
Published in North America by Chronicle Books, San Francisco.
Printed in Spain.

Chronicle Books
85 Second Street
San Francisco, CA 94105

http://www.chronbooks.com

Distributed in Canada by
Raincoast Books
8680 Cambie Street
Vancouver B.C. V6P 6M9